Out of the Water

A Baptism Devotional

by Marya Patrice Sherron

This devotional was inspired by a former student. Many years after her graduation, Torri continues to check on me regularly and asks how she can pray for me. If you have a Beautiful spirit in your life like Torri, you are indeed blessed.

All scriptures are in the New International Version.

An Imprint of KI Productions, LLC

Copyright © 2023 by Marya Patrice Sherron

All rights reserved.

Printed in the United States of America
ISBN: 978-1-961605-04-6

First Edition

Written, Designed, & Edited by Marya Patrice Sherron

This journal belongs to:

_____

Hello Family,

Baptism is a special act & public confession of our faith in Jesus Christ. We do this as a symbol of cleansing, burial, and new life. Some consider Baptism as a place marker for their spiritual journey.

Most significant is that our savior challenged his disciples to confess their faith before others (Matthew 32:3; 16). Jesus' last instruction is also noteworthy, "Go therefore and make disciples of all nations, baptizing them in the name of the Father and of the Son and of the Holy Spirit, teaching them to observe all that I have commanded you. And behold, I am with you always, to the end of the age." (Matthew 28:18-20)

Congratulations on your Baptism. May this devotional journal bless you in the days ahead. Study, pray, reflect, and listen to the Holy Spirit within.

Love & Prayers Always,
Marya

Truths To Stand On

There is profound
beauty in a life
glorifying God.

Our Lord loves you.

Prayer is powerful &
effective.

Our Lord is with you
and will not forsake
you.

Our Lord is our source
of rest & strength.

Lord, today I seek your guidance and pray in the name of Jesus...

Date:

_____

_____

_____

_____

_____

_____

_____

_____

_____

_____

_____

_____

Date:

What verse will you commit to memorizing?

Date:

_____

_____

_____

_____

_____

_____

_____

_____

_____

_____

_____

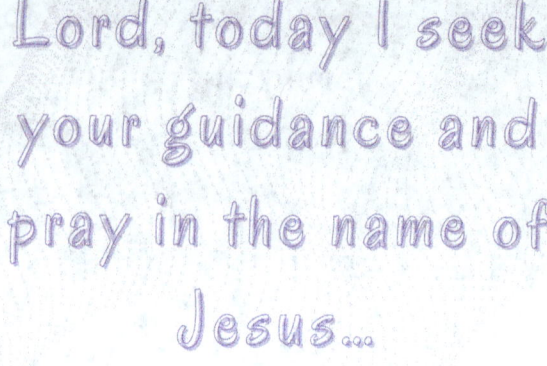

Lord, today I seek your guidance and pray in the name of Jesus...

Date:

_____

_____

_____

_____

_____

_____

_____

_____

_____

_____

_____

Date:

*I can do all this through him who gives
me strength.*

Philippians 4:13

Date:

_____

_____

_____

_____

_____

_____

_____

_____

_____

_____

Lord, today I seek
your guidance and
pray in the name of
Jesus...

Date:

_____

_____

_____

_____

_____

_____

_____

_____

_____

_____

_____

Date:

"Baptism is faith in action."

Watchman Nee

Date:

_____

_____

_____

_____

_____

_____

_____

_____

_____

_____

_____

_____

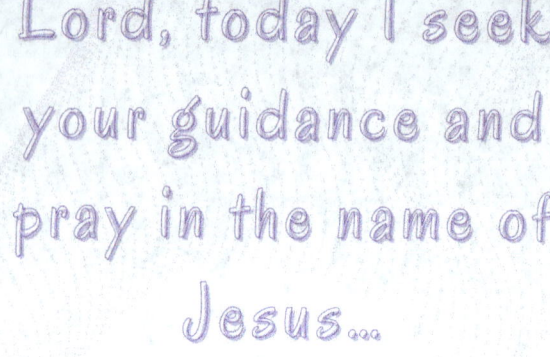

Lord, today I seek
your guidance and
pray in the name of
Jesus...

Date:

_____

_____

_____

_____

_____

_____

_____

_____

_____

_____

Date:

For God so loved the world that he gave his one and only Son, that whoever believes in him shall not perish but have eternal life.

John 3:16

Date:

Lord, today I seek your guidance and pray in the name of Jesus...

Date:

_____

_____

_____

_____

_____

_____

_____

_____

_____

_____

_____

_____

Date:

Whoever believes and is baptized will be saved, but whoever does not believe will be condemned.

Mark 16:16

Date:

_____

_____

_____

_____

_____

_____

_____

_____

_____

_____

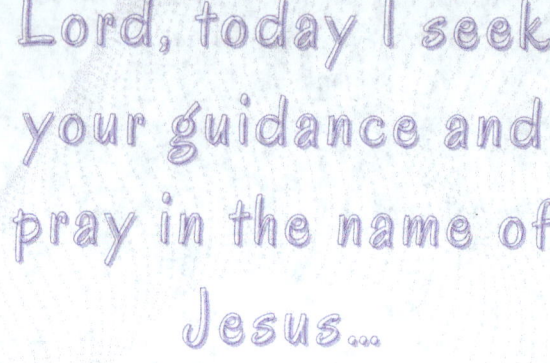

Lord, today I seek
your guidance and
pray in the name of
Jesus...

Date:

_____

_____

_____

_____

_____

_____

_____

_____

_____

_____

_____

Date:

Date:

Lord, today I seek
your guidance and
pray in the name of
Jesus...

Date:

_____

_____

_____

_____

_____

_____

_____

_____

_____

_____

_____

_____

Date:

Practice taking the time
to reflect on all you are
grateful for and recognize
answered prayers.

Date:

_____

_____

_____

_____

_____

_____

_____

_____

_____

_____

_____

Write your memory verse above.

Habits to Develop

Read & Reflect on the Holy Scripture as a way of life.

Talk to God often without creating a rigid process.

Memorize verses and recite them often.

Ask for wisdom & scriptural understanding.

Always have a spiritual mentor.

Ask others how you can lift them in prayer.

Practice lifting others in prayer immediately rather than saying, "I'll pray for you."

Be Still.

Listen to the sound of silence.

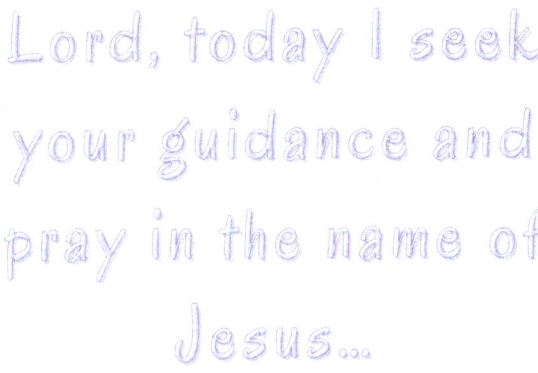

Lord, today I seek
your guidance and
pray in the name of
Jesus...

Date:

_____
_____
_____
_____
_____
_____
_____
_____
_____
_____
_____

Date:

What verse will you commit to memorizing?

Date:

_____

_____

_____

_____

_____

_____

_____

_____

_____

_____

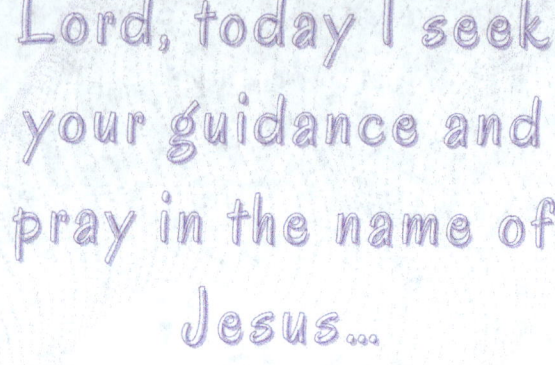

Lord, today I seek
your guidance and
pray in the name of
Jesus...

Date:

_____

_____

_____

_____

_____

_____

_____

_____

_____

_____

_____

Date:

Wait for the Lord;
be strong and take heart
and wait for the Lord.

Psalm 27:14

Date:

_____

_____

_____

_____

_____

_____

_____

_____

_____

_____

Lord, today I seek
your guidance and
pray in the name of
Jesus...

Date:

_____

_____

_____

_____

_____

_____

_____

_____

_____

_____

_____

_____

Date:

He says, "Be still, and know that I am God;
I will be exalted among the nations,
I will be exalted in the earth."

Psalm 23:4

Date:

_____

_____

_____

_____

_____

_____

_____

_____

_____

_____

_____

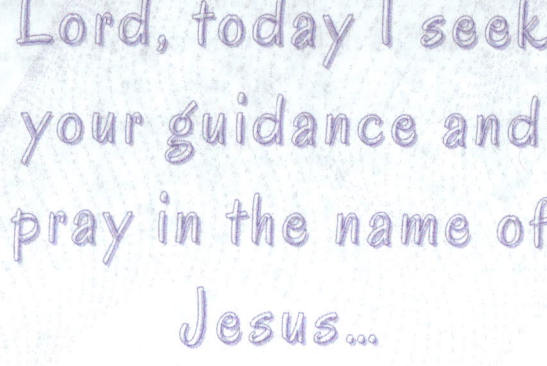

Lord, today I seek
your guidance and
pray in the name of
Jesus...

Date:

_____

_____

_____

_____

_____

_____

_____

_____

_____

_____

_____

Date:

You intended to harm me, but God intended it for good to accomplish what is now being done, the saving of many lives.

Genesis 50:20

Date:

_____

_____

_____

_____

_____

_____

_____

_____

_____

_____

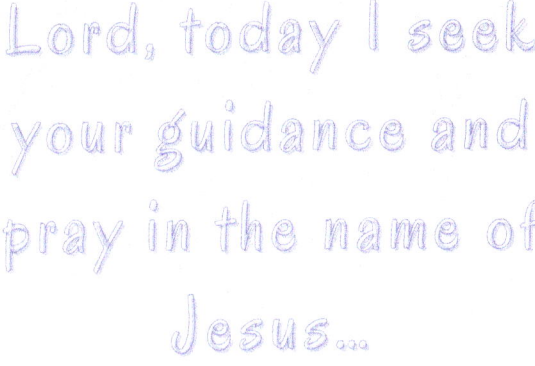

Lord, today I seek your guidance and pray in the name of Jesus...

Date:

_____
_____
_____
_____
_____
_____
_____
_____
_____
_____
_____
_____

Date:

But seek first his kingdom and his righteousness,
and all these things will be given to you as well.
34 Therefore do not worry about tomorrow, for
tomorrow will worry about itself. Each day has
enough trouble of its own.

Matthew 6:33-34

Date:

_____

_____

_____

_____

_____

_____

_____

_____

_____

_____

_____

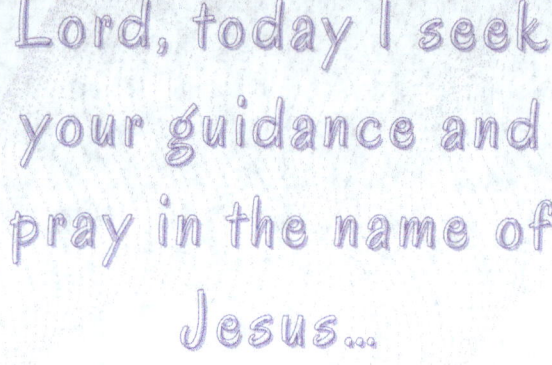

Lord, today I seek
your guidance and
pray in the name of
Jesus...

Date:

_____

_____

_____

_____

_____

_____

_____

_____

_____

_____

Date:

Date:

_____

_____

_____

_____

_____

_____

_____

_____

_____

_____

_____

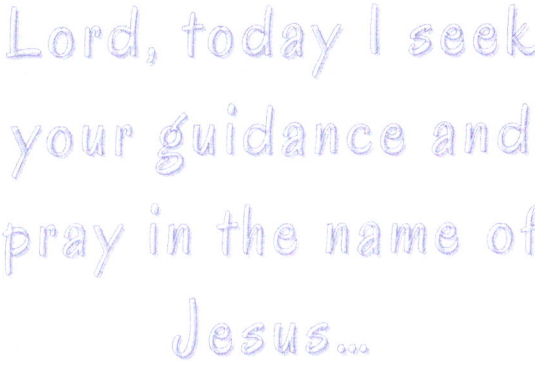

Lord, today I seek
your guidance and
pray in the name of
Jesus...

Date:

_____

_____

_____

_____

_____

_____

_____

_____

_____

_____

_____

Date:

Practice taking the time
to reflect on all you are
grateful for and recognize
answered prayers.

Date:

_____

_____

_____

_____

_____

_____

_____

_____

_____

_____

Write your memory verse above.

"Thorns are Little things,
'Things that prick, penetrate
... and progressively poison.
Unexpected things.
Low-lying vines that trip, tangle
... and eventually imprison."

Charles Swindoll

Know your thorns and present them to our Lord.

Find your special place to spend
time alone with our Lord
regularly.

Listen Within

Allow the presence of peace in your heart to guide you.

The Holy Spirit lives in you.

There are times you need only be still.

Some battles are not ours—but our Lord's.

There is a time to Do Nothing.

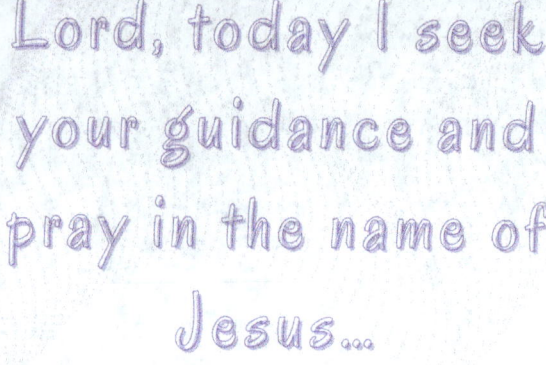

Lord, today I seek
your guidance and
pray in the name of
Jesus...

Date:

_____
_____
_____
_____
_____
_____
_____
_____
_____
_____
_____

Date:

What verse will you commit to memorizing?

Date:

_____

_____

_____

_____

_____

_____

_____

_____

_____

_____

Lord, today I seek your guidance and pray in the name of Jesus...

Date:

_____

_____

_____

_____

_____

_____

_____

_____

_____

_____

_____

Date:

So those who received his word were baptized, and there were added that day about three thousand souls.

Acts 2:41

Date:

_____

_____

_____

_____

_____

_____

_____

_____

_____

_____

_____

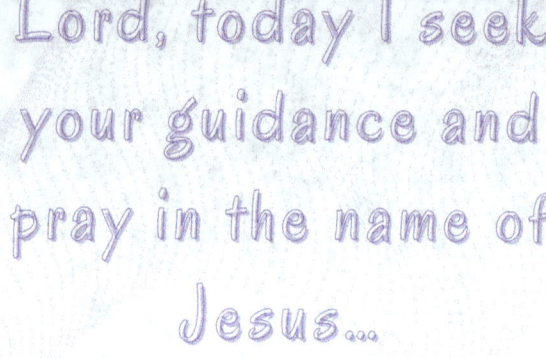

Lord, today I seek
your guidance and
pray in the name of
Jesus...

Date:

_____

_____

_____

_____

_____

_____

_____

_____

_____

_____

_____

Date:

And we know that in all things God works for the good of those who love him, who have been called according to his purpose.

Romans 8:28

Date:

_____

_____

_____

_____

_____

_____

_____

_____

_____

_____

Lord, today I seek your guidance and pray in the name of Jesus...

Date:

_____

_____

_____

_____

_____

_____

_____

_____

_____

_____

_____

Date:

He has shown you, O mortal, what is good.
And what does the Lord require of you?
To act justly and to love mercy
and to walk humbly with your God.

Micah 6:8

Date:

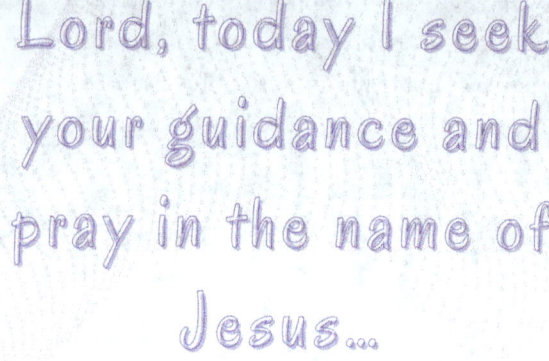

Lord, today I seek
your guidance and
pray in the name of
Jesus...

Date:

_____
_____
_____
_____
_____
_____
_____
_____
_____
_____
_____

Date:

Now when all the people were baptized, and when Jesus also had been baptized and was praying, the heavens were opened, and the Holy Spirit descended on him in bodily form, like a dove; and a voice came from heaven, "You are my beloved Son; with you I am well pleased."

Luke 3:21-22

Date:

_____

_____

_____

_____

_____

_____

_____

_____

_____

_____

Lord, today I seek your guidance and pray in the name of Jesus...

Date:

_____

_____

_____

_____

_____

_____

_____

_____

_____

_____

_____

Date:

Date:

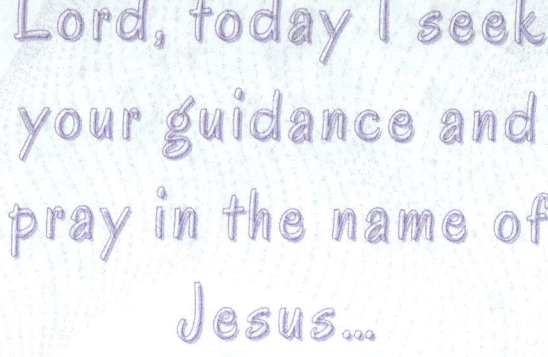

Lord, today I seek
your guidance and
pray in the name of
Jesus...

Date:

_____
_____
_____
_____
_____
_____
_____
_____
_____
_____
_____

Date:

Practice taking the time
to reflect on all you are
grateful for and recognize
answered prayers.

Date:

_____

_____

_____

_____

_____

_____

_____

_____

_____

_____

What do you see in this image?

_____

_____

_____

Write your memory verse above.

Misunderstood

Your faith will be misunderstood by many—remain strong & courageous.

Be bold & loving in sharing your faith.

Do not argue.

Let others see your faith in Action, not Words.

Seek wisdom & give abundantly.

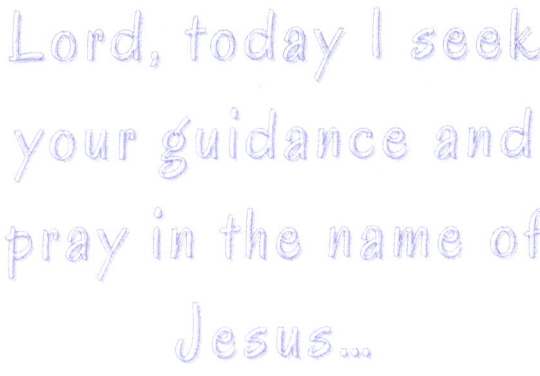

Lord, today I seek
your guidance and
pray in the name of
Jesus...

Date:

_____

_____

_____

_____

_____

_____

_____

_____

_____

_____

_____

_____

Date:

What verse will you commit to memorizing?

Date:

_____

_____

_____

_____

_____

_____

_____

_____

_____

_____

_____

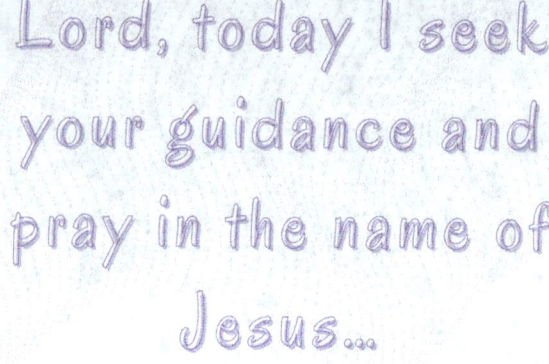

Lord, today I seek
your guidance and
pray in the name of
Jesus...

Date:

_____

_____

_____

_____

_____

_____

_____

_____

_____

_____

Date:

And my God will meet all your needs
according to the riches of his glory in Christ
Jesus.

Philippians 4:19

Date:

_____

_____

_____

_____

_____

_____

_____

_____

_____

_____

_____

Lord, today I seek
your guidance and
pray in the name of
Jesus...

Date:

_____

_____

_____

_____

_____

_____

_____

_____

_____

_____

_____

Date:

"At Baptism, I received grace — that quality that makes me share in the very nature of God."

Mother Angelica

Date:

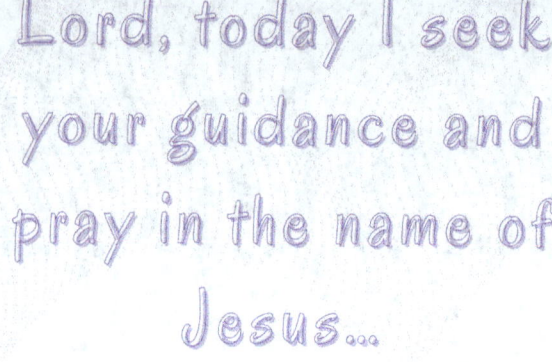

Lord, today I seek
your guidance and
pray in the name of
Jesus...

Date:

_____

_____

_____

_____

_____

_____

_____

_____

_____

_____

Date:

Go therefore and make disciples of all
nations, baptizing them in the name of the
Father and of the Son and of the Holy
Spirit, teaching them to observe all that I
have commanded you. And behold, I am with
you always, to the end of the age.

Matthew 28:19-20

Date:

_____

_____

_____

_____

_____

_____

_____

_____

_____

_____

Lord, today I seek your guidance and pray in the name of Jesus...

Date:

Date:

So from now on we regard no one from a worldly point of view. Though we once regarded Christ in this way, we do so no longer. 17 Therefore, if anyone is in Christ, the new creation has come: The old has gone, the new is here! 18 All this is from God, who reconciled us to himself through Christ and gave us the ministry of reconciliation.

2 Corinthians 6:16-18

Date:

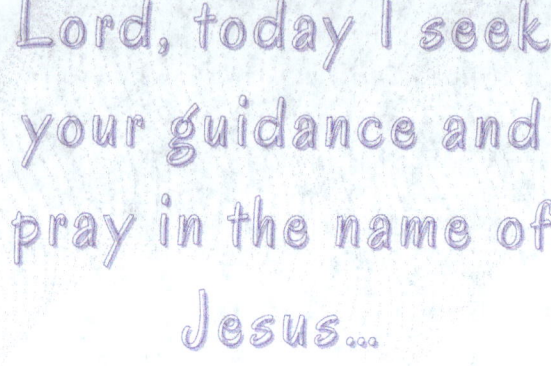

Lord, today I seek
your guidance and
pray in the name of
Jesus...

Date:

_____
_____
_____
_____
_____
_____
_____
_____
_____
_____
_____

Date:

Date:

_____

_____

_____

_____

_____

_____

_____

_____

_____

_____

_____

Lord, today I seek
your guidance and
pray in the name of
Jesus...

Date:

_____
_____
_____
_____
_____
_____
_____
_____
_____
_____
_____
_____

Date:

Practice taking the time
to reflect on all you are
grateful for and recognize
answered prayers.

Date:

_____

_____

_____

_____

_____

_____

_____

_____

_____

_____

_____

_____

Write your memory verse
above.

Power of Seasons

Winter is sure to
come, but so is spring.

Hope will guide you
through dark seasons.

You have the strength
to endure.

Grow to understand
our Lord's sense of
Time, not man's.

Awake grateful each &
every day.

Patience

&

Love

Grow Beautiful Creations

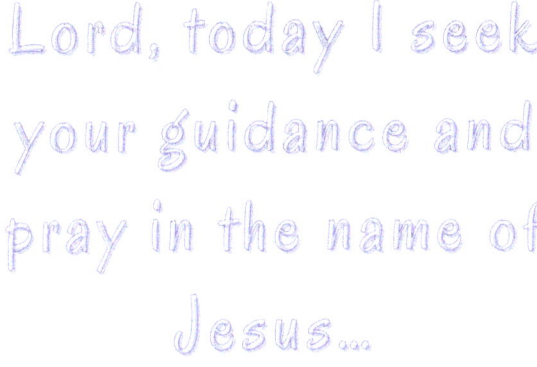

Lord, today I seek your guidance and pray in the name of Jesus...

Date:

_____

_____

_____

_____

_____

_____

_____

_____

_____

_____

_____

Date:

What verse will you commit to memorizing?

Date:

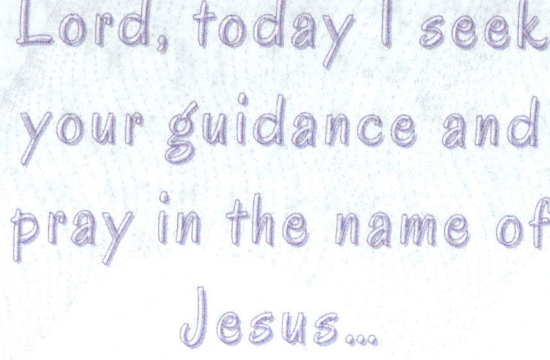

Lord, today I seek
your guidance and
pray in the name of
Jesus...

Date:

_____

_____

_____

_____

_____

_____

_____

_____

_____

_____

_____

Date:

And this water symbolizes baptism that now saves you also—not the removal of dirt from the body but the pledge of a clear conscience toward God. It saves you by the resurrection of Jesus Christ.

1 Peter 3:1

Date:

_____

_____

_____

_____

_____

_____

_____

_____

_____

_____

Lord, today I seek
your guidance and
pray in the name of
Jesus...

Date:

_____
_____
_____
_____
_____
_____
_____
_____
_____
_____
_____
_____

Date:

Having been buried with him in baptism, in
which you were also raised with him through
your faith in the working of God, who raised
him from the dead.

Colossians 2:12

Date:

_____

_____

_____

_____

_____

_____

_____

_____

_____

_____

_____

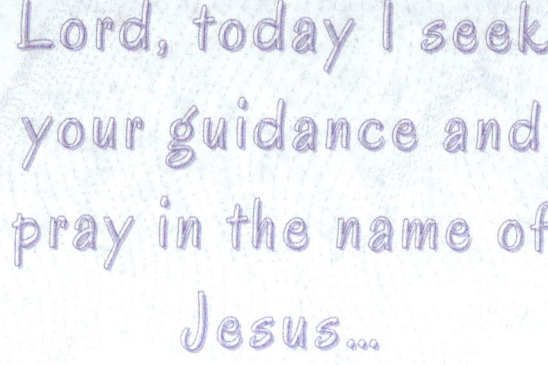

Lord, today I seek your guidance and pray in the name of Jesus...

Date:

_____

_____

_____

_____

_____

_____

_____

_____

_____

_____

_____

Date:

Even though I walk
through the darkest valley,
I will fear no evil,
for you are with me;
your rod and your staff,
they comfort me.

Psalm 46:10

Date:

Lord, today I seek
your guidance and
pray in the name of
Jesus...

Date:

_____
_____
_____
_____
_____
_____
_____
_____
_____
_____
_____
_____

Date:

Do not be anxious about anything, but in every situation, by prayer and petition, with thanksgiving, present your requests to God. 7 And the peace of God, which transcends all understanding, will guard your hearts and your minds in Christ Jesus.

Philippians 4:6-7

Date:

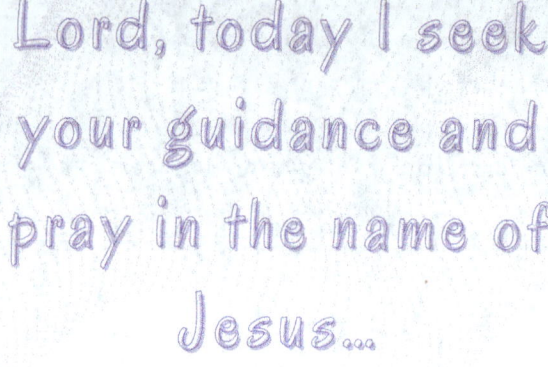

Lord, today I seek
your guidance and
pray in the name of
Jesus...

Date:

_____

_____

_____

_____

_____

_____

_____

_____

_____

_____

Date:

Date:

_____

_____

_____

_____

_____

_____

_____

_____

_____

_____

Lord, today I seek your guidance and pray in the name of Jesus...

Date:

_____

_____

_____

_____

_____

_____

_____

_____

_____

_____

_____

Date:

Practice taking the time
to reflect on all you are
grateful for and recognize
answered prayers.

Date:

_____
_____
_____
_____
_____
_____
_____
_____
_____
_____
_____

Write each
of your
memory
verses
below.

Date:

My Baptism

Date:

_____